Daft Doughnut

About the Author

Adrian Mitchell is one of today's leading poets and playwrights for adults and children. For his popular poems, and his amazing poetry performances all over the world he has been named the Shadow Poet Laureate. Adrian was born in London near Hampstead Heath and educated by wolves. His books for Orchard include *Balloon Lagoon* and *Zoo of Dreams, The Orchard Book of Poems, Dancing in the Street, A Poem a Day* and *The Adventures of Robin Hood and Marian*.

'I cannot think of a better living English poet to lead young readers into the magic rooms of poetry's enchanted palace.' Carol Ann Duffy

Daft as a Doughnut contains poems published in *All Shook Up* (Bloodaxe), *Blue Coffee* (Bloodaxe), *Gynormous!* (Orion), *Nobody Rides the Unicorn* (Doubleday), *The Pied Piper* (Oberon), *The Snow Queen* (Oberon), *With Love* (Orchard), *Balloon Lagoon* (Orchard) and *Zoo of Dreams* (Orchard).

ORCHARD BOOKS
96 Leonard Street, London EC2A 4XD
Orchard Books Australia
32/45-51 Huntley Street, Alexandria, NSW 2015
ISBN 1 84362 685 3 (paperback)
First published in Great Britain in 2004
Text © Adrian Mitchell 2004
Illustrations © Tony Ross 2004
The rights of Adrian Mitchell to be identified as the
author and of Tony Ross to be identified as
the illustrator of this work have been asserted by them in
accordance with the Copyright, Designs and Patents Act, 1988.
A CIP catalogue record for this book is available from the British Library.
1 3 5 7 9 10 8 6 4 2
Printed in Great Britain

Daft as a Doughnut

ADRIAN MITCHELL

Illustrated by TONY ROSS

ORCHARD BOOKS

GOOD LUCK, TEACHERS!
Please don't use these poems or any
of my other work in exams or tests.
But I'm happy if people choose to read
them aloud, learn them, sing, dance
or act them in or out of school.

**Dedicated with all my love
to my grandchildren –**

Natasha

Charlotte

Caitlin

Arthur

and Annie

Lola

Zoe

Robin

CONTENTS

3. ONLY KIDDING

4. ALL AROUND THE WORLD

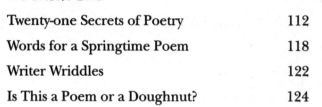

7. POETRY D.I.Y.

1
Come
On In

Daft as a Dougnut

Happy as a holiday
Grumpy as a grown-up
Potty as a poet's day
Daft as a doughnut

Bloated as a big balloon
When it's being blown up
Jazzy as a jungle moon

Daft as a doughnut

How to Write Poems

Bite your lower lip,

Stick out your tongue.

That's the way

The poems get done.

Screw up your eyes,

Take a new look.

That's the way

Poems start to cook.

A Poet's Life for Me

"Are you the Author Dude?" – small American boy
just before my poetry performance in Seattle.

I was born wearing jeans and an invisible hat,
With the heart of a mouse but the rhythm of a cat.

At eight I stowed away on a pirate vessel
Sailing over the Ocean of Dreams
And there I was taught how to write, rhyme and wrestle
By a mermaid selling hot ice-creams.

At eighteen I was a tramp in the City of Trees
And studied in a College of Chimpanzees.
I learned How To Dance The Banana Fling,
How To Doze On A Branch and How To Swing.

But now I run a Poetry Corner Shop
Selling Fizzy Crisps and Cheese And Onion Pop,
And I write for kisses and I write for kicks –
So come on in – mix and match and pick and mix!

2
Animals Forever!

Animal

My Favourite Word

My favourite word is Animals –
The plural, not the singular,
For in that one word Animals,
How many miracles there are.

Mrs Christmas

She was about as small as a cup
But big as your head when she grew up
And she came to stay on Christmas Day
So we called her Mrs Christmas

She liked to swoop around the hall
With a silver paper soccer ball
And I think I was four but maybe some more
When I named her Mrs Christmas

She had some kittens with bright white socks
And she kept them in a brown cardboard box
And she'd nudge them out and march them about
Saying:

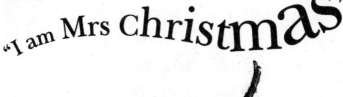

"I am Mrs Christmas"

Dog Bog

I know a dog
His name is Josh
In the **muddy muddy** bog
Josh likes to s p l o s h
When I say Josh
You need a wash
He says By gosh
I don't want to be posh
I want to splosh splosh splosh
In the **muddy muddy** bog
All day

I know a dog
Her name is Trish
In the **muddy muddy** bog
Trish likes to splish
When I say Trish
You're not a fish
She says Oh pish
It's my only wish
I want to splish splish splish

In the muddymuddy bog
All day

I know a dog
Her name is Sash
In the muddymuddy bog
Sash likes to splash
When I say Sash
The bog's full of trash
She says Balderdash
It's a lovely mish-mash
I want to splash splash splash
In the muddymuddy bog
All day

splosh splosh splosh goes my friend Josh
splish splish splish goes my friend Trish
splash splash splash goes my friend Sash
splash splish splosh
In the muddymuddy bog
All day

Disguise

Every morning after I shampoo my fur
I climb into my humanskin costume and
Put on my human mask and human clothes
Then I go out into the human city
And catch a human bus to work

As I sit at my computer
Summoning up images of the
    financial world
None of my colleagues know
That inside my human hand gloves
Are the brown and burly
Sharp and curly
Paws of a grizzly bear

Yes, I am a bear in a cunning disguise,
Only passing as human
Trying not to yield to temptation
As I lumber past
The sticky buns in the baker's shop
The honeycombs in the health shop

I am married to a human woman who knows
    my secret
We have a human daughter
Who is rather furry and has deep golden eyes
And gentle paws
We call her Bruinhilda

I took Bruinhilda to a circus once
But there was a performing bear
Riding a unicycle, juggling with flames
Dancing to an accordion

I sat tight
Though she might have been my mother
I sat tight
While the inside of my human mask
Filled up with the tears of a bear

There's No Business Like Slow Business

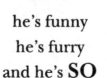

A Snail named Maurice
met a Slug called Doris

off to the forest
crawled Maurice and Doris

to watch a show
by Boris the Slow
Loris
for Maurice and Doris
love Boris the Loris

he's funny
he's furry
and he's **SO**

s l o o o o o o o o o o o o o w

The Pelican

The sunset glows
Like the inside of a peach
I see a pelican
Standing on the beach
The pelican looks
So clumsy and sad
I want to take him home
To my mum and dad
But he shakes his long beak
And jumps into the skies

Away he flies

And graceful as an angel

Gorillas

Moonlight upon the mountains
And the gentle Gorillas awake

They lumber along through the forest
To sit by the side of the lake

And there in the silvery water
They dangle their ticklish toes

And what the Gorillas are thinking
Nobody nobody knows

The Arrival of the Seal

Tailfin churning like an outboard motor
He charges through the ice floe and up the shore
He toots for his mate with his boot-polished hooter
And a million diamonds shine all over his fur

Nobody Rides
the Unicorn

His coat is like snowflakes
Woven with silk.
When he goes galloping
He flows like milk.

His life is all gentle
And his heart is bold.
His single horn is magical
Barley sugar gold.

Nobody rides the Unicorn
As he grazes under a secret sun.
His understanding is so great
That he forgives us, every one.

Nobody rides the Unicorn,
His mind is peaceful as the grass.
He is the loveliest one of all
And he sleeps behind the waterfall.

To See a Unicorn

This is the way to see a Unicorn:

Close your eyes.

See a sandy path in front of you.
Follow that path over a hill of grass and daisies.

Take a deep breath.
See a bumpy little stream in front of you.

Follow that stream into a forest.
Take a deep breath.

See a clearing in the forest
And a pool like a mirror for the trees.

Take a deep breath.
Be still.

Who walks so gracefully down to the pool
And bends to drink the cool dark water?

It is the Unicorn, the loveliest of animals.
He loves to wander in the forest of your dreams.

See his silver mane and his golden horn.
See his gentle eyes.
Hear the beating of his heart.

Be still.

Open your eyes
When you want to open your eyes.

Remember the Unicorn.

Welcoming the Birds

You hold up your hand.

Now your hand's a tree.

Small birds fly to it

Gratefully

And they rest their wings,

Your sweet-singing friends,

As they perch like snowflakes

On your fingers' ends.

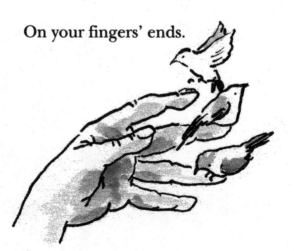

Henry the Golden Retriever

Ten months old
Same colour as the sunshine

Over the grass he jumps

His only fault
Is bumping into you
But they are friendly bumps

All the Animals Gathered Round

Guitar in his hand
Leaning on an Elephant
Orpheus sings

A Wolfhound and St Bernard
At his knees

A grey Ox
Cocks his ear

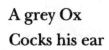

Two Swans
Lift their snaking heads
Towards the music

The Geese are paddling in the shadows
Gathering peppery green weeds

A flowering Ostrich on a rock
Throws back her wings
In ecstasy

The Waterfall bounces
Silver notes

A Leopard reclining
Like a streamlined blonde

A Lion and Lioness
Roll their golden eyes

A Heron taking off
On a journey to the hidden stars

The Peacock flaunts
His starry blue
Waterfall of a tail

A million Birds
In proud mid-flight
Scattering their colours
All over the sky

A lurking Buffalo
With guilty eyes

A family of Deer
Guarding each other with their branches
Birds and Animals

Feeding   Drinking   Singing   Resting

The Trees are dancing
Stretching and swirling
And the Sky is a dance
Of speeding blue and white

It is all a dance
And at its centre
The wedding of two Horses
They have a special temple
Of grass and flowers
Among the shining rocks

The Grey Horse looks at us
The Chestnut turns away
Their flanks are touching
Silver flank against
Chestnut flank

Two Horses
So glad and close together
It can only be love

Never lose it

Guitar in his hands
Leaning on an Elephant
Orpheus sings

*(Orpheus was such a great singer that when he sang all the animals,
both wild and tame, gathered round him. This poem is a description
of a beautiful painting, by Roelant Savery, in the Fitzwilliam Museum,
Cambridge. It's a very small, bright, crowded picture and you
have to look carefully to find Orpheus and the Elephant
up in the top right-hand corner.)*

Gubblefish Soup

Take a one-eyed frog
From a bubbling bog
Rub him down with talcum powder
Feed a kidney cake
To a rattlesnake
And then pound him into chowder
Pour them in a dish
With some jellyfish
Boil them up till they're delicious
Don't be cautious
Add a pair of galoshes
And a bunch of gubblefishes

Gubblefish gubblefish gubblefish soup
Your eyebrows jump
Your whiskers droop
Your guts go **boing!**
And you loop the loop
With gubblefish gubblefish gubblefish soup

Take a dozen pails
Full of giant snails
And a fried Egyptian mummy
Melt a telescope
With a bar of soap
That'll make the mixture yummy
Stir 'em up with glue
To a steamy stew
And squash 'em till they squishes
That's a jumbo
Kind of mumbo gumbo
And it tastes like – gubblefishes

Gubblefish gubblefish gubblefish soup
Your eyebrows jump
Your whiskers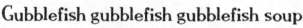
Your guts go boing!
And you loop the loop
With gubblefish gubblefish gubblefish soup

Fights I Have Fighted

When I fought a Boa Constrictor –
I licked 'er.

In a battle with a Cheetah –

I easily beat her.

But when I saw an Axolotl –

I lost me bottle.

Electric Advice

Never take
A bath in the dark.
You might use the wrong flannel

or sit on a shark.

3
Only
Kidding

Sticky-up Hair

I've got _{sti}cky-u^p hair
I've got _{sti}cky-u^p hair
Like a tuft of grass
On top of a hillock.

I've got _{sti}cky-^{out} teeth
I've got _{sti}cky-^{out} teeth
But they don't make me
Look like a pillock.

Doing the
Best I Can

Dad
showed me
my new
half-sister.

I love Dad
so I
half kissed her.

Just Me

My name is Benjy
I am three
I want to walk downstairs –
    Just me.

Out in the street
I want to be
I'll catch a bus –
    Just me.

I'll drive that bus
Over the sea
To a magic island –
    Just me.

I'll live in a hut
In a monkey tree
Eating chocolate parrots –
    Just me.

Then I'll make a plane
And fly off to see
The African Jungle –

Just me.

I'll meet an elephant
Called Tennessee.
I'll ride on his back –

Just me.

He'll carry me home
Across the sea.
I'll shout: "I'm back
With Tennessee!"

We'll drink a mug
Of elephant tea,
Then we'll clump upstairs –
Tennessee and me.

He can sleep
In the lower bunk
So I can reach down
To pat his trunk.

And I'll tell him about
How it used to be
When I had no elephant friend –

Just me.

It Came from Under the Table

It came from under the table
During one of Grandpa's speeches.
We heard its movements down below
Like the squelch of rotten peaches.

It came from under the table
With the scent of forgotten cheese
But first it chewed on our toenails
And then it nibbled our knees.

O its clammy touch
Was much too much –
Father dashed off to work
Gran hid herself
On the teapot shelf
And the rest of them went berserk.

Yes it came from under the table
Like a phantom from the sea.
But I was the scaredest one of all –

Was I It? Or was It me?

To Caitlin Riding on my Shoulders

When you're up there
High in the air
Riding upon my shoulder
You play with my hair
Like it's some kind of rare
White grass growing
On an old pink boulder

Don't you know I'm underneath
With my detachable teeth
Thinking how wonderfully wild you are
So hang on tight
Pull my scalp off that's all right
Your ever-loving Grandpapa

In Mrs Moon's Class

I write words down on paper
I fit them in between the lines
The paper is white
The lines are light blue

Straight rivers in rows
On oblong fields of snow

I look up at the blackboard
Wide night sky
With a few white speck stars

My teacher's face is the moon
The moon is white
The moon is very far away

I do not know what the moon
   thinks
The moon is bright
The moon does not know
   what I think so

I write words down on paper

Sunset Verse

The setting sun is like an orange

Writes our poetic teacher, Lucy.
So where's the pips, yells Billy Cripps,
Why isn't the sun juicy?

A NOTICE TO STICK
UP ON THE DOOR
OF YOUR ROOM
If Sneaky-Snoop
Comes sniffing around
Something really horrible
Will always be found

The Sadness of
a Giant Child

I'm four years old.
I'm eight feet high.
They take me to a little school
And leave me to cry.

The grown-ups laugh.
The children scream.
I feel like a hairy
Monster in a dream.

Our teacher is a Tiny.
We call her Miss Priscilla.
Her favourite fairy story
Is Jack the Giant-Killer.

I sit in the corner
Like a wardrobe to sulk.
The other kids call me
The Inedible Hulk

And the only time they let me
Join in a game
Is when I let them use me
As a climbing frame.

So each night I pray
To the God of the Tall:
"Please, Lord, let me
Grow up to be small."

Lighting Up Time

you're afraid of the dark
you try to be brave
you screw up your eyes
so you can't see the dark

but you can still feel
how the dark fills your room
you can still feel
the dark on your face
and you're afraid of the dark

don't be afraid
I will stand beside your bed
and hold up both my hands
and stretch my fingers
and each finger shall be
a bright-dancing candle
filling your room with gentle light

so don't be afraid of the dark
and I'll stand by your bed
to shine away the dark
every night until you say
go away now go away
I'm not afraid of the dark any more

Little Lola
Demonstrates Tai Chi

like this:
her right arm rises
slowly   gently

like this:
her fingers unfold
slowly   gently

her fingers fold
her right arm falls
slowly   gently

like this:
her left arm rises
slowly   gently

like this:
her fingers unfold
slowly   gently

her fingers fold
her left arm falls
slowly   gently

and it is just like walking down
a winding
sandy path
through a mystery garden

just like walking down
to a deep and greeny pool
and seeing
for the first time in your life

a water-lily

4
All
Around
the World

The Wildest Wheelbarrow in the World

It's a Cadillac Subaru Bullnose Lada
With GBH overdrive
It's a Formula Zero
Robert de Niro
The most weed-unfriendly barrow alive
It's got rally-bred CD
Yes indeedy
With a DVD of solid steel
Yes it's the Wildest Wheelbarrow in the World
And it's riding on a wonky wheel

It's the Wildest Wheelbarrow in the World
I never saw another like that
So switch on the telly
And give it some welly
We'll be round the world in eighty seconds flat

It's a woodentop Jaguar Jumback Dolby
With hot and cold data base
It's stereo diesel
Runs like a weasel
With a spookerama smile all over its face

It's got a luxury fountain
A microfiche mountain
With cotton-picking reel-to-reel
Yes it's the Wildest Wheelbarrow in the World
And it's riding on a wonky wheel

It's the Wildest Wheelbarrow in the World
It's proof against bullets and spears
It's chromium-plated
Decaffeinated
And guaranteed for seven thousand years

It's the Wildest Wheelbarrow in the World
I never saw another like that
So switch on the telly
And give it some welly
We'll be round the world in eighty seconds flat

It's the Wildest Wheelbarrow
Wonderfullest Wheelbarrow
Wickedest Wheelbarrow
In the wide wide wide World!

One of the First Poems to be Written Underneath the English Channel or maybe The First

The bones of galleons and their wide-eyed crews,
Haunted by jelly-fish and purple mussels –
They're overhead, stuck in historic ooze –
As our train mumbles through the dark to Brussels.

THE RETURN JOURNEY

As our train mumbles through the dark from Brussels,
They're overhead, stuck in historic ooze –
Haunted by jelly-fish and purple mussels –
The bones of galleons and their wide-eyed crews.

(This historic poem was written on October 16th 1996 while riding the Eurostar Train, carriage 16, seat number 76, during the twenty minutes in which we travelled through the Chunnel. After ten minutes I realised I could cover the journey home by reversing the order of the lines. Dedicated to the staff and pupils of the British School at Brussels.)

October

I could eat October
drink its bonfiresmoke
spread my marmalade coloured wings
and walk up the stairs of the sky

I love October leaves
who know better than anyone
how to die happily –
turn pale green
fade to yellow
burn to red
or brown
or gold

then
let go
and
see-saw lightly
down to
where the leaves lie
whispering excitedly
about the bonfire

Blackberry Picking Song

The green little, mean little, lean little berries
Are always at the bottom of the blackberry bush
But the biggest best berries are always high
On the branches way up in the sky.

Though the brambles may scratch
We jump and we hop
For we have to snatch
The ones at the top

Yes, the green little, mean little, lean little berries
Are always at the bottom of the blackberry bush
But the biggest best berries are always high
On the branches way up in the sky.

And those berries we'll cart
Back home to our mam
For blackberry tart
And blackberry jam

For the biggest best berries are always high
On the branches way up in the autumn sky
For blackberry tarts! And blackberry jelly!
And blackberry jam! And wonderful blackberry pie!

Moondog in New York

There was a man called Moondog
Who made tunes
With thimbles, glasses, zithers,
Keys and spoons
And all the tunes he made
Were living things

Which flew around his head On silver wings

I bought a Moondog record
Fourteen tracks
A red and golden label
Dusty wax
The sounds were delicate
As cowrie shells
The moonlit dancing
Of a thousand bells

My first day in New York
I walked downtown
Moondog sat on the sidewalk
All in brown
He played his instruments
So sweet and wild
I wanted to stay with him
As his child

Aladdin's Palace

The walls of the Palace are golden
With diamond windows
And ivory doors
Its halls are high
As the sapphire sky
And panthers prowl across
The marble floors

There are courtyards with meadows and rivers
Where hummingbirds hover
And unicorns run
The lofty towers
Stand like shining flowers
And slender minarets
Point to the sun

An oakwood dinner table five miles long
Laden with silver plates
Of pheasants and salmon
Welsh rabbit and gammon
And pancakes, cherries and chocolate dates
  In the magical Palace

A deep blue swimming pool that's wide and warm
Palm trees and waterslides
And ice cream and peaches
And long surfing beaches
And a dolphin to take you for white-knuckle rides
  Round the magical Palace

A lake where elephants and hippos swim
And a gorilla tree
Spaniels and foxes
A pool room, juke boxes
And a shopping mall where everything's free –

Down in a studio your favourite band
Plays while you sing along
There are trampolines
All sorts of magic machines
And comical robots which never go wrong
    In the magical Palace

And when you're tired of all this glory
You'll retire to a four-poster bed
Carved angels and dragons
Will sing you a story
Till you dream of the one you'll wed
    In the magical Palace
In the magical Palace of your dreams

Riding West from The Little Bear

I ride a horse called Secrets
A lively dapple-grey
His hoofbeats echo down the trail
They call the Milky Way

Past a stampede of meteors
Down the ravines of space
And over deserts of silver dust
Watchfully we pace

We journey on with hopeful hearts
Though the way's long and far
But sometimes halt and light a fire
Upon some lonesome star

Moonbathing

All kinds of bathing
Make the body happy
Your mind goes mellow
And your toes turn tappy
Bathing makes your heart bounce like
a rubber ball
But Moonbathing is the best of all

Well I know
Sunbathing is the game to play
Feel your troubles all melting away
Mud bathing's an odd way to wash
But it's fun as you squish and squash

River bathing is a special treat
If there's no crocodiles after your feet
Honey bathing is sticky but fun
You have to take a steam bath after that one

Yes all kinds of bathing
Make the body happy
Your mind goes mellow
And your toes turn tappy
Bathing makes your heart bounce like
a rubber ball
But Moonbathing is the best of all

Silver beams
Slowly pouring over you
Silver dreams
Are soaring over you
Moon bathing
Dream bathing
Drinking in the light
Of the magical moon
Moonbathing is the best of all!

In a Japanese City

she is a maker
of tissue paper flowers

gently she bends their petals
pink and blue and ivory
into light blossom patterns

she makes little flowers
they are no bigger than her eyes

approximately roses
approximately daffodils
but never exactly
and sometimes invented flowers
or flowers picked from her
summertime dreamfields

she makes tissue paper flowers
and scatters them secretly
by ones or by twos
in unexpected places

on a train seat
or a briefcase
on the bonnet of a car
or the brilliant surface of a puddle

she lets drop
one or two
and they drift
towards the ground
and she is out of sight
around the corner
long before they land

paper kingcups
or buttercups
they sit and wobble
and balance and toboggan
on the small breezes
of the grimy air

she took a basket
of a thousand blossoms
to the top of a tower
in the middle of the city
she emptied them into
a passing cloud and
watched them drift
over streets and schools
and parking lots

a thousand blessings
on the city

Green Dungarees

When I'm invited to a posh party
Or my teacher's dropping round
Or I should be sloshing up
The washing up
I'm never to be found.
And when my uncles start to get hearty
Or I broke a window pane
Or it's time for addition
Or a composition
I've disappeared again –

I climb into my
Green dungarees
And I put on my
Heavy duty
Garden boots
And I vanish myself
Beyond the trees
    And I'm planting shoots
And pulling up roots

And the sun shines down
Like an old yellow cheese
On me at my work
In my green dungarees

Gardening's peaceful when you're on your own
Every now and then you may think a thought
But once in a while I invite a friend
A gardening friend who's not the talkative sort

We climb into our
Green dungarees
And we put on our
Heavy duty
Garden boots
And we vanish ourselves
Beyond the trees
And we're planting shoots
And pulling up roots

Till the stars shine down
Like bright sweet peas
On me and my friend
In our green dungarees...

5
Magic Journeys

Who

who invented the moon?
a drop of milk from a porridge-eater's spoon
some ragamuffin from the back of beyond
lifted the lid off a frozen pond
sprinkled it with mashed up mother-of-pearl
and hung it up to stare at the sleepy world
who invented the moon?
some muddlesome young buffoon
stole a princess's silver crown
put it in a cauldron and melted it down
dipped a marble in the molten and soon
out it popped as the moon

who invented the moon?
maybe a rabbit from a TV cartoon
wanted to play soccer with a blonde baboon
they stole some ice cream – vanilla –
from a drowsy old gorilla
and froze it round a blue balloon
and there was the moon
there was the moon
there was the dear old moon

A Lost Princess

In the rusty murk
In the musty dark
A long boat slides
Along the lake

And at its prow
Stands the Lost Princess
With moondust scattered
On her midnight balldress

Through a battered brass telescope
The Sad Pirate watches her disappear
And his face turns into a marble rock
And his heart to a starry tear

The Mucky Princess

The mucky Princess
  liked to play in the mud
she would wallow and roll and dig

The mucky Princess
  loved the mud so much
she found a new job as a pig.

A Surprise Parcel

Hairy green string
Blobs of purple sealing-wax
Six postage stamps bearing silver holograms
Of the Snow Queen on an iceberg throne
Muddy brown wrapping paper
Round a soggy heavy cardboard box
When you sway it from side to side
You hear a swishing-swashing sound

Somebody has sent you a river

The Quest of the Deep-Freeze Knight

My armour is wafers
My helmet's a cone
As I fearlessly march
Through the Ice-cream Zone

I journey on
Towards my duty
Through the bright Forest
Of Tutti Frutti

Past Strawberry Hill
And Vanilla-Tree
I keep my mind chill
And military

Then under a bush
Of Pistachios
I trim my ferocious
Moustachios

Then I don silver boots
And onwards I trudge
Over the Desert
Of Chocolate Fudge

Will I see
From some far and fatal ridge –
Cassata Castle
And the King of the Fridge?

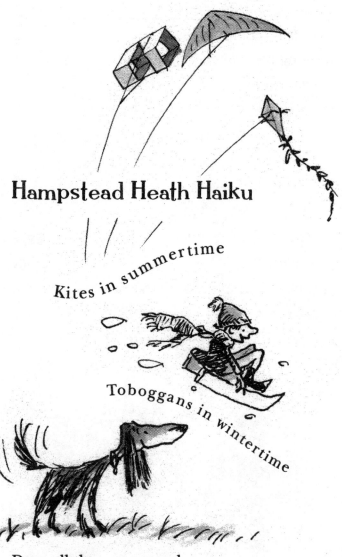

Hampstead Heath Haiku

Kites in summertime

Toboggans in wintertime

Dogs all the year round

My Lost Dog

You were lost in my dream
I was looking for you everywhere
Somebody told me to try the station
It looked like you on the railway bridge

The railwaymen had turned their signal box
Into a wooden restaurant
They cooked in bright red buckets which said FIRE
But the inside of their buckets were polished gold

You were lost in my dream
I was looking for you anywhere
I was just going to cry when I woke up –
    And here you are

Secret Country *(from The Pied Piper)*

There is no money
So there's no crime
There are no watches
'Cos there's no time
It's a good country
It's a secret country
And it's your country and mine

If something's needed
You make it there
And we have plenty
For we all share
It's a kind country
It's a secret country
And it's your country and mine

There are no cages
There is no zoo
But the free creatures
Come and walk with you
It's a strange country

It's a secret country
And it's your country and mine

There are no prisons
There are no poor
There are no weapons
There is no war
It's a safe country
It's a secret country
And it's your country and mine

And in that country
Grows a great tree
And it's called Freedom
And its fruit is free
In that blue country
In that warm country
In that loving country
In that wild country

In that secret country
Which is your country and mine

6
Daft as a Doughnut

Some Sad Story

I am Fred
My head
Is made of bread

I lay down
Beside a pond
Along come
A quacker and a swan

Hey!
Where's my bread head gone?

CRUMBS!!!

Good Old Mud

Poets and mud
Attract each other
For poets know
Mud was our Mother.

Great things are done
When mud and poets meet
But nothing good is done
In Oxford Street.

I Saw Two Ghosts

I saw two ghosts when I was six
Two ghosts in one night

The first ghost was a small squat woman
Almost a cube shape
Head like a squashed box
Her mouth a dark pillarbox slot

And then I slept

The second ghost came when I woke again
Standing where the woman had stood
The second ghost was a big square butcher
Holding a huge mallet
Looking both pleased and savage
Obviously the man who flattened Little Boxhead

But when daylight came
I saw the two of them
Reduced to a wooden wardrobe
With luggage stacked beside it

My terror laughed itself away

Nowadays I'm not scared of ghosts
        But I'm terrified of wardrobes

The Giant's Love Song

Oh my love's enormous, just like me,
And just like me, she's true
And her eyes are like two basketballs
If basketballs were blue.

When my darling whispers in my ear
It is like a blunderbuss
And my love is dainty to be seen
As St Pancras Terminus.

Oh her face is like the scarlet sun
When the tropical sunset falls
And her breast is like Mount Everest
And her dome is like St Paul's.

Yes, her hair is like a forest fire,
Like a glowing tower her nose
And her teeth stand in her mighty gums
Like tombstones in two rows.

Her knees are like two pyramids
When she's lying very still
And her foot is like a river barge
And her bottom's like Primrose Hill.

Oh my love's at least one hundred times
As big and fair as you.
Yes, my love's enormous, just like me.
And just like me, she's true.

Backhead

This morning I woke up with a grunt
To find my head was on back to front

A Warning to Those who Fly

If you break wind in outer space
The gas that you expel
May freeze into a solid mass –
A planet made of smell

And living creatures may evolve
To praise with all their heart
The great creator of their home,
The fragrant Planet Fart.

Ancestor Maths

You were born from
    two parents
and four grandparents
who were born from your
    eight great-grandparents
who came from your
    sixteen great-great-grandparents
who were produced by your

    thirty-two great-great-great grandparents
about 240 years ago.
Now they came from your
    sixty-four great-great-great-great grandparents
who were born to your
    128 great-great-great-great-great grandparents
who issued from your
    265 great-great-great-great-great-great
grandparents descended from your

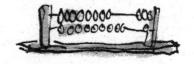

512 great-great-great-great-great-great-great
    grandparents
around 540 years ago.
But they didn't come from nowhere they came
    from your
1,024 great-great-great-great-great-great-
great-great grandparents
who sprang from your
2,048 great-great-great-great-great-great-
great-great-great grandparents
who were the children of your
4,096 great-great-great-great-great-great-
great-great-great-great grandparents
who were created by your
8,192 great-great-great-great-great-great-
great-great-great-great-great grandparents
    say 720 years ago.

Well, they must be the offspring of your
    16,384 great x12 grandparents
born to your
    32,768 great x 13 grandparents
made by your
    65,536 great x 14 grandparents
produced by your
    131,072 great x 15 grandparents
    who thrived about a thousand years ago –
    say 1,000 AD approximately.
So their mothers and fathers were your
    262,144 great x 16 grandparents
spawned by your
    524,288 great x 17 grandparents
who must be the children of your
    1,048,576 great x 18 grandparents
born and raised by your
    2,097,152 great x 19 grandparents
maybe one thousand two hundred and forty
       years ago.
To cut a long story shortish you had
4,194,304 great x 20 grandparents,

8,388,608 great x 21 grandparents,
16,777,216 great x 22 grandparents
33,554,432 great x 23 grandparents
67,108,864 great x 24 grandparents
134,217,728 great x 25 grandparents
268,435,456 great x 26 grandparents

like, 1,640 years ago.

And – you had
536,870,912 great x 27 grandparents
1,073,741,824 great x 28 grandparents
2,147,483,648 great x 29 grandparents
4,294,967,296 great x 30 grandparents
8,589,934,592 great x 31 grandparents
17,179,869,184 great x 32 grandparents
exactly two thousand years ago…

hey!

just a minute!
hangaboutabit!

Two thousand years ago the population of
the world
was only 200 million people.
But you had 17 billion, 179 million,
869 thousand 1884
super-great grandparents hanging around at
the time.
Doesn't add up.

We have a problem.

17,179,869,184 minus 2,000,000

seems to me to equal

16,979,869,184 grandparents who just
   weren't there.

Seems to me that 16,979,869,184 of

your incredibly great grandparents –

MUST HAVE
COME FROM
OUTER SPACE!

Wrong Planet Blues

Born on the wrong planet
But I do the best I can
This is not my planet
But I do the best I can
Wake up early every morning
Disguise myself as a man

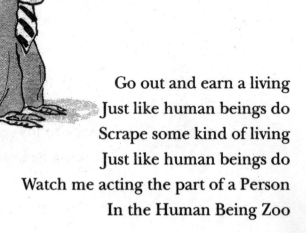

Go out and earn a living
Just like human beings do
Scrape some kind of living
Just like human beings do
Watch me acting the part of a Person
In the Human Being Zoo

Born on the wrong planet
But I'll be going home some day
This is not my planet
I'll go home some sweet day
The skeleton rocketship
Coming to fly me away

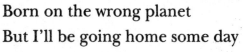

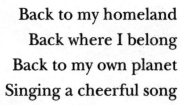

Back to my homeland
Back where I belong
Back to my own planet
Singing a cheerful song
Back to a planet that feels right to me
Even when I'm doing wrong

On my Rooftop

Bounding
resounding
a massive stream
a shuddering
flood
surrounded by steam

too warm to be snow
too wild to be rain
it must be that weak-bladdered
Giant again
that ogre in a toga
that gynormous goof –

PIDDLER ON THE ROOF!

What's a Basin?

A basin means
You have a hot lake when you want one
And a cold lake when you want one –
A lake big enough
For your hands to go swimming in.

When your hands are tired of swimming
Take them out and shake them.
Your hands make rain.
Then you yank out the plug

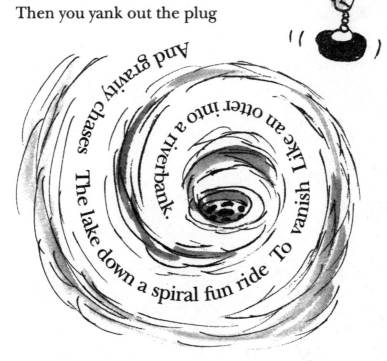

And gravity chases The lake down a spiral fun ride To vanish Like an otter into a riverbank.

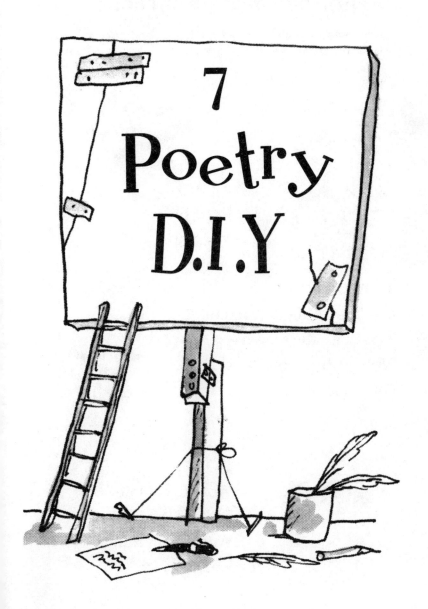

7
Poetry
D.I.Y

Twenty-one Secrets of Poetry

(Every art and craft and sport and skill has its Secrets. Here are some of the Secrets I've learned which may help you write your own poems)

One
Use your feet
To find the beat

Two
If the old word won't do
Make up a new

Three
Don't write about Autumn
'Cos that's the season –
Write your poems
For a real reason

Four
Write to cool down
Write to get hot
Write about things
You like a lot

Five

Write for other people;
Quite a few
Will sit down and write
A poem for you

Six

Like a poppy-field poppy
Be happy to copy

Seven

Good ideas often fly off, and so
Take that notebook wherever you go
  (and three pens)

Eight

Rhyme Time ime Pime?

You can rhyme every time at the end of a line
And that's no crime if the words feel fine,
But on the other hand you can write a poem
Which doesn't have any rhymes at all

Nine

What can you write about?
It helps very much
If you choose something
You can see and touch

Ten

Maybe the search for food,
Maybe a quest for glory,
But write a poem
Which tells a story

Eleven

Pile up your feelings
On a poetry plate –
Write about something
You really hate

Twelve

To make a poem
That lasts a minute
Daydream for hours
Before you begin it

Thirteen

Don't just write
For the literate few –
Write for babies
And animals too

Fourteen

When you read to a friend
Or recite to a crowd
Say your poem
Slow and loud

Fifteen

Poetry's a lovely, dangerous game
But it's very unlikely to bring you fame
So don't try to live by your poetry
You'd earn more selling cat food on Mercury

Sixteen

Sad poems, funny poems –
Feel everything you're writing.
Rough poems, gentle poems –
Make them all exciting

Seventeen

It's pretty tiring
Just being you –
Write from other people's
Points of view
Use lots of different voices and you may
End up with a poem
That becomes a play

Eighteen

All you can do with
    your life
Is live it
Poetry's a gift –
So give it

Nineteen

If you want to learn
How to talk to grass
Or dance the giraffe
Or imitate glass
Invite a poet
Into your class

Twenty

Write a secret poem
That you never show
Learn it and burn it
So nobody will know

Twenty-One

These are Secrets.
None of them are Rules
Here's another Secret:
There are no Rules in poetry

*(Except the ones you make up for yourself
Which you can break whenever you like.)*

Words for a Springtime Poem

adoring

adorning

alarming

alerting

charming

charring

chirruping

churning

coursing

courting

dairying

dallying

exerting

emerging

ferrying

flirting

glorying
glowing
harrying
hurrying

marrying
mourning

piercing

querying

shirting
skirting
slurring
slurping
smarting
smirking
snarling
snorting
sparking
sparring
sporting
spurning
spurring
spurting

starling
starring
starting
starving
sterling

stirring
storming

swarming
swerving
swirling

tarrying
twirling

wearying
whirling

yearling
yearning

Z PRING!

Writer Wriddles

The Tale of Eat A Rabbit by Beatrix Rotter

The Tale of Jemima Crispyduck by Beatrix Hotter

Harry Potter and the Tenpins of Fire
by J K Bowling

The Adventures of Huckleberry Hound
by Bark Twain

Robinson Floppyears by Spaniel Defoe

The Sowman by Raymond Piggs

Charlie and the Curry Factory by Tarka Dal

Sticky Island by Robert Gluey Stevenson

Alice in Beerland by Lewis Barrel

The Merchant of Jelly by William Shakespoon

The Tragedy of Macbeef by William Steakspeare

The Loaftrap by Agatha Crusty

Phoney-O and Juliet by William Fakespeare

Big Fat Dorrit by Charles Thickens

Bleak Coop by Charles Chickens

The Merchant of Tennis
   by Wimbledon Shakespeare

A Midsummer Night's Insomnia
   by William Wakespeare

The Canterbury Cups by Geoffrey Saucer

Paradise Cheese by John Stilton

The Song of Lowerwatha by Shortfellow

Body in Toytown by Enid Frighten

Animal Hospital by George Unwell

The Illustrated Bum by Jacqueline Wilmoon

The Lunchpack of Notre Dame by Pizza Tugo

The Big Spot of the Baskervilles
   by Arthur Conan Boil

The Ghoul and the Vampirebat Went To Sea
   by Edward Fear

Is this a Poem or a Doughnut?

When is a Poem a Doughnut,
Asks the ancient riddle?
When it can roll and it has a big hole
Or a blob of red jam in the middle.

You may say mine are as fresh as a daisy
Or dry as a dinosaur bone,
But if you don't fancy my doughnuts like crazy –
Bake your own!

The End

Index of First lines